WHEN IN DOUBT, LEAD!

The Leader's Guide To Enhanced Employee Relations In The Fire Service

▲

By

Dennis Compton

Published by

Fire Protection Publications

Oklahoma State University

Editing and layout by Jerry Laughlin

ISBN 0-87939-165-0
Library of Congress #99-60152

First Edition
Printed in the United States of America

10   9   8   7   6   5   4   3   2

Contact us for more information about Fire Protection Publications at Oklahoma State University, headquarters of the International Fire Service Training Association:

  Send email to *editors@osufpp.org*
  Phone (405) 744-5723
  Write to 930 North Willis, OSU, Stillwater, OK 74078
  Or see our web page at *www.ifsta.org*.

Contents

Dedicated to:

Sher, Michelle, and Barry for their support and encouragement.

Alan Brunacini, Pat Cantelme, Gary Pykare, Harold Mace, and many others for helping me with a host of lessons.

Introduction

IT IS DIFFICULT TO IMAGINE a more important issue in the workplace than employee relations. The way that the work-force (labor) and management interact has a direct impact on the quality of the service or product, and thus, the bottom line. This provides more than ample reason to pay a lot of attention to it, whether you work in a fire department or other organization.

In many organizations, this relationship is less positive and effective than it could be. In fact, in most of those same organizations, the leadership of the labor group and management wish it could be more productive, but they lack a guide for changing the relationship. Doing so requires significant commitment and the setting aside of traditional roles and approaches to dealing with each other. It also includes finding commonalities in agendas and a process to help labor and management leaders work through issues rather than arrive at a conflict-guided stalemate.

There is not a creditable leader in labor or management who hasn't wished for something better, a process geared toward mutual trust, mutual respect, problem solving, and even joint planning.

There is good news, because there is a way to make such a relationship a reality. It requires strong leadership, hard work, and a commitment to take a risk with each other. Sometimes it's a lot easier to just keep fighting.

The purpose of this book is to describe a road map to a more successful relationship between labor and management leaders. I know it's possible, because I've been involved with fire departments that have taken the journey…together. No matter what the current relationship, improving it can help the bottom line, for customers, employees, and managers. It will also improve the quality of internal and external service. There can't be better reasons to proceed.

I hope you find the book interesting and the growth of your organization exciting.

Connecting the Organization

W E ALL GO TO CONFERENCES and seminars to gather information, meet people in our field, and learn about specific programs that are being proposed (or that are in place) in other organizations. We might have taken an idea home only to find that the framework was not in place to allow it to be effective in our own fire organizations.

There are growing pains involved with development that cannot always be transferred. Organizations sometimes need to tailor change to their own culture and environment in order for it to be successfully implemented. There are organizational anchors that can be developed to enhance the change process. These anchors can be critical to improving overall effectiveness. They also help to connect support staff to line personnel, management to firefighters, and performance to positive outcomes.

The following appear to be some of the most critical of these organizational components. They are presented in the form of questions so that you can evaluate whether or not they've been addressed in your organization, and to what degree. They are not in any order of importance because each is interdependent upon the others.

This is not intended to be an all-inclusive list, but I think it represents some of the key organizational elements necessary to operate effectively together.

Fire departments functioned in groups or teams long before it became vogue to do so. There are departments that seem to be able to shift, grow, and change, and there are those that for some reason cannot. One of the keys to stability and security in today's work-world is flexibility and adaptability. Without something to hold onto (such as these key anchors), fire departments can find themselves committed to yesterday and drifting towards a world that no longer exists. We are all subject to falling into this leadership trap.

Answer the questions in this chapter for your organization. Identify the strengths and weaknesses and make them areas of focus so that the organization might become more effective. We should be proud of our traditions and our past…and we shouldn't let go of the things that are key to our effectiveness.

Key Organizational Elements

	Yes	No

▸ Is the focus of the effort and energy extended by the people in the organization directed towards providing an exceptional product and/or quality customer service (externally and internally)?

▸ Are the mission and values of the organization documented and shared in a meaningful way?

▸ Are the mission and values referenced periodically by the organization?

▸ Is there an *organizational structure* that clearly defines roles and areas of responsibility?

▸ Is there an *operational structure* that displays how the organization functions on a daily basis?
(Sometimes these two structures are the same, but many times they are not.)

Key Organizational Elements

	Yes	No

▶ Is there a planning process that provides long-term and short-term direction to the members and policy-makers?

▶ Is the planning document kept current, and is it regularly referenced?

▶ Are there times when joint planning and problem solving occur within the labor/management relationship?

▶ Or is the typical mode of interaction confrontational?

▶ Is quality leadership present in both groups?

▶ Is there decentralized budget development and administration that seeks member involvement at various levels of the organization?

▶ When teams or committees are established, is participation a positive organizational experience?

Key Organizational Elements

	Yes	No
▸ Does team or committee participation too often result in frustration and unresolved conflict?	___	___
▸ Do managers utilize some system for program management to ensure that objectives are established and progress measured and reported?	___	___
▸ Is there a priority placed on trying to improve overall communications in all directions throughout the organization?	___	___
▸ Does the organization provide tools and forums that help with this communications process?	___	___
▸ Is there a sense of commitment by the individual members to the organization's mission?	___	___
▸ Are managers committed to supporting the people who produce the product and/ or provide the service?	___	___

Key Organizational Elements

☑

Yes   No

▸ Do members at each organizational level know what's expected of them in terms of communications and working together?

▸ Do members at each organizational level have sufficient latitude to perform and are they accountable for outcomes?

▸ Are the culture and philosophy of the organization defined so that both can be more effectively communicated and evaluated?

This information helps identify and define the environment in which activities occur in an organization. The more we learn about the environment, the more effective we can become at developing relationships and processing issues and change. Perhaps your answers to these questions will help you develop a plan designed to hold onto the strengths, change as necessary, and progress towards tomorrow.

Committees and Teams:

Helping Them Be More Effective

Chapter
Two

GOOD ORGANIZATIONS are made up of capable and committed people who try to stay focused on external and internal service delivery. They use groups (or teams) to research issues and make decisions that guide several programs and projects. This process can be a very positive tool in an organization, or it can create significant dissension and frustration among the members who participate. One of the factors that dictates which effect it will have is how much guidance and leadership is provided to the teams when they are initially established and as they go about their work.

Using team processes does not eliminate conflict (nor should it), and it does not represent an easier way of doing business and making decisions. Many times it takes longer using the group, but the process usually results in better decisions for the fire department.

Some fire departments have restructured their committees and instead follow more of the team approach that we have seen in some of the more current management models that organizations are using. It really doesn't matter what the groups are called (committees or teams); what matters is that they have the leadership and guidance necessary to be effective.

Team Profile

A tool that can help is the team profile. It is a short document that must be completed, communicated internally, and kept current for all standing teams (ongoing) and project teams (special purpose) that are constituted in an organization.

The documents are maintained by a specified manager, but they are completed by each team under the guidance of the chair and the sponsor.

All teams should utilize agendas, action plans, and publish minutes of their meetings in an effort to make the process as open and effective as possible.

The team profile requires that the following information be decided and communicated before the team starts its work:

- The name of the team.
- A narrative describing the scope of the team's work.
- The name and work assignment of the team sponsor. (This is the manager who will help guide the work of the group).
- Team facilitator or chair(s) name and work assignment.
- Team recorder name and work assignment.

- A determination as to whether the group is a standing team or project team? (If project team, list duration)
- The frequency and location of meetings
- A list of the team members
- Any special team instructions or predictable parameters.

This tool does not guarantee successful committees or teams, but it certainly helps improve the odds. A few other things to keep in mind include:

▶ Management should never constitute a team to review and rubber-stamp an issue on which the final decision has already been made. This is patronizing to the team members.

> Being members of teams encourages people to participate in decisions that relate to their work and/or issues on which the organization is seeking their input.

▶ The team's recommendation may not be exactly what management would have done, but it may be just as good (or better). There is more than one right way to go about something. Don't discard the work of the team over insisting on changing a few details that would probably work just as well anyway.

▶ Be certain that the scope and parameters are defined as clearly as possible. If the team's work is going to be used in an advisory capacity that may be significantly refined by management later, tell them so up-front.

...continued on page 14

Team Profile

The following profile must be completed, communicated, and kept current for all Standing and Project Teams that are constituted in the organization.

Name of team:

_____

Scope of team's work:

_____

_____

_____

_____

_____

_____

Team sponsor:

_____

Name   Division

Team facilitator or chair:

_____

Name   Work assignment

Team recorder:

_____

Name   Work assignment

Check one: ☐ standing team   or   project team ☐

_____

Duration of assignment, if project team

Frequency and location of team meetings:

_____

Team members:

_____   _____

_____   _____

_____   _____

_____   _____

_____   _____

_____   _____

_____   _____

_____   _____

Special instructions or predictable parameters for this team (if any):

_____

_____

_____

_____

_____

▶ Being members of teams encourages people to participate in decisions that relate to their work and/or issues on which the organization is seeking their input. It doesn't set anyone up as being in a position to dictate policy or work outside the scope of the team. If a team is drifting away from their scope, or operating outside of the parameters that were established, the sponsor and/or chair(s) should redirect their efforts.

Teams can be an effective way to involve people in the department and create positive settings where sound, functional decisions can be made. They enhance a sense of ownership and help foster responsibility and accountability within the organization. Perhaps this simple tool will be of assistance to others who are committed to making the team process work.

Employee Relations
Evaluation and Improvement Tool

Chapter Three

EMPLOYEE RELATIONS PLAYS A CRITICAL role in the overall effectiveness of an organization. Whether a fire service, sales, manufacturing, or other work force, the ability of managers and workers to interact cooperatively is in the best interest of all involved, including the customers. The quality of the internal environment, especially in the service industry (and the fire service is a service industry), is no secret to the external customers. At times the customers are actually victimized by dysfunctional internal relationships.

Before we can change our course, it is sometimes helpful to define the current state of the relationship. The following evaluation and improvement tool is designed to assist in determining the current status of employee relations in a particular organization. Leaders of management and those from labor could complete this tool in an effort to define the current state of employee relations in the organization, and use the results as a starting point for the future.

Introduction

The purpose of the questions making up this evaluation and improvement tool is to assist in defining the current level of interaction and involvement among labor and management leaders within your organization, then to encourage the joint development of action plans designed to define and establish the desired relationship for the future. The instructions will clearly guide you through the completion of this tool.

Behavioral Definitions for Assessment

Read each of the behavioral elements on the following pages and mark the number below each one (1, 2, 3, or 4) that corresponds to your evaluation of the specific behavior in your organization.

Evaluation Scale

Evaluate and rate each of the behaviors within this tool utilizing the following scale:

1 This behavior **almost never** occurs in my organization.

2 This behavior **periodically occurs** (although sometimes reluctantly) in my organization.

3 This behavior **is usually a goal** of labor and management leaders in my organization.

4 This behavior **occurs regularly** and defines the labor/management leadership focus in my organization.

Rating the Current Status

▶ Labor and management leaders understand the types of work they do well together and use the roles of labor and management creatively to achieve the goals of the organization. Results are not accomplished at the expense of each other.

▶ The leadership of labor and management keep their word by doing the things that they say they are going to do.

▶ Labor and management leaders put the collective good of the organization as a whole above the good of either labor or management, or the individual leaders of each group.

▶ The formal contract (where one exists) is a very important component of the labor/management process, but it does not drive the relationship.

▶ The leaders of labor and management meet on a scheduled basis to conduct joint planning and problem-solving utilizing action plans that are codeveloped and monitored for progress.

▸ Labor and management leaders realize that there will be disagreements on certain issues. The leadership is able to proceed with issues on which there is agreement while continuing to communicate on areas where disagreement exists.

▸ Labor and management leaders value the importance of maintaining an open, productive relationship. Neither party's leadership would sacrifice the overall labor/management relationship to achieve a single outcome on a specific issue.

▸ Labor and management leaders are committed to (and focus on) the importance of providing the highest quality of service or product possible to the external customers.

▸ Labor and management leaders are committed to (and focus on) the importance of providing the best support possible to the organizations members…the internal customers.

▸ When the organization is struggling, labor and management leaders work together to navigate and survive the difficult period and find opportunities for improvement as a result of the event or situation.

▸ Management leaders share the authority for decision-making and creating the vision and policies of the organization.

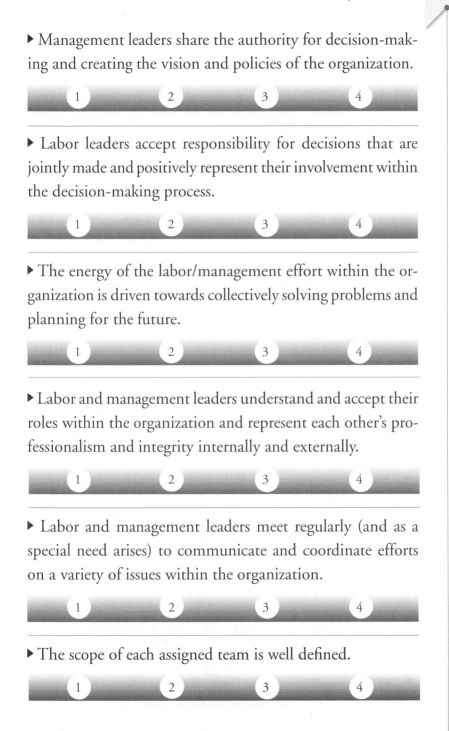

| 1 | 2 | 3 | 4 |

▸ Labor leaders accept responsibility for decisions that are jointly made and positively represent their involvement within the decision-making process.

| 1 | 2 | 3 | 4 |

▸ The energy of the labor/management effort within the organization is driven towards collectively solving problems and planning for the future.

| 1 | 2 | 3 | 4 |

▸ Labor and management leaders understand and accept their roles within the organization and represent each other's professionalism and integrity internally and externally.

| 1 | 2 | 3 | 4 |

▸ Labor and management leaders meet regularly (and as a special need arises) to communicate and coordinate efforts on a variety of issues within the organization.

| 1 | 2 | 3 | 4 |

▸ The scope of each assigned team is well defined.

| 1 | 2 | 3 | 4 |

▶ Labor and management leaders cooperatively participate on committees or teams assigned to address issues within the labor/management process.

▶ Labor and management leaders are proactive when addressing issues that typically lead to grievances. Complaints by members are communicated and processed within the organization.

▶ Labor and management leaders focus their efforts on planning and problem-solving, while also discussing culture, policy, and defining procedures.

▶ It is understood by both parties that the labor leaders manage the day-to-day operations of the employee group, and management leaders manage the day-to-day operations of the organization…and that each conducts business within the scope of the policies and procedures that have been jointly developed.

Your Results

Add the total number of your responses in each of the following levels and enter them below:

Level	Characteristic	Number of Responses
1	Confrontational	_____
2	Armed Truce	_____
3	Interactive	_____
4	Cooperative	_____

Characteristics of the Four Levels of Labor/Management Relations and Involvement

Read the following characteristics and descriptions. Based upon your total responses to each, identify the current level at which you have rated your organization's labor/management relationship:

Confrontational

In the confrontational relationship, the roles of labor and management leaders are rigid and adversarial. Labor and management view each other as competitors, and there is an underlying distrust and lack of respect, which limits communications. The negotiated contract (where one exists) is the focus of their interaction, which is usually win/lose driven in an atmosphere where grievances are encouraged. Leaders take advantage of each other in bad times and the organization is preoccupied with its negative history.

Armed Truce

In the armed truce relationship, the roles of labor and management leaders are rigid, but there is some constructive communication that occurs. Many times, the relationship has moved from confrontational to armed truce due to damage the two groups have done to the overall organization, which created the motivation for both parties (labor and management) to survive and do no additional harm to each other. Although labor and management leaders begrudgingly admit that both groups have rightful roles, the relationship is fragile and drives an us/them approach to doing business. Labor and management leaders struggle with each other during bad times. Meeting together is mostly issue-driven and grievances occur frequently.

> In the armed truce relationship, the roles of labor and management leaders are rigid, but there is some constructive communication that occurs.

Interactive

In the interactive relationship, labor and management leaders have accepted each other's roles in the overall effective operation of the organization. Both parties stress the importance of providing quality services or products to the external customers and acknowledge the importance of the members of the organization in achieving the mission. Labor and management leaders meet periodically to enhance communications and solve problems. There is some level of joint participation on committees and both parties tend to approach surviving bad times together. A degree of organizational forgiveness exists to excuse and forget the problems of the past. Complaints from members of the organization receive attention. There are periodic grievances.

Cooperative

In the cooperative relationship, labor and management leaders utilize each other's roles in a way that is function based rather than ego based, and they are directed towards what's best for the organization as a whole. There is a high level of trust and respect that has been mutually earned, and the relationship between the labor and management leaders is valued throughout the organization. The focus of leadership is on the quality of services and/or products delivered externally and the support of the members of the organization internally. Power, control, and influence are infused throughout the organization. Management shares its authority for decision-making, and labor accepts responsibility for its role in the decision-making process. There are regular meetings that involve communications, problem-solving, and planning for the future, but the leadership of both parties focus on culture, policies, and procedure development, avoiding the inclination to co-manage the day to day activities of the organization through committees. The leaders have developed the ability to agree to disagree on some issues, yet continue to

> The focus of leadership is on the quality of services and/or products delivered externally and the support of the members of the organization internally.

work on other unrelated issues. Labor and management leaders work jointly to seek opportunities that present themselves during, and as a result of, bad times. Smart risk-taking is encouraged and managed. Grievances are rare.

Conclusion

Based upon the total number of your responses within each level of the employee relations and involvement model, determine where your labor and management leadership has taken the overall relationship in your organization. Utilize the definitions provided within this tool for assistance in ascertaining the key elements of your specific organizational situation.

> As a result of this exercise, the users could choose to develop specific action plans to modify the labor/management relationship.

As a result of this exercise, the users could choose to develop specific action plans to modify the labor/management relationship. The action plans should include specific objectives, time frames, and the responsible persons. A facilitator might be required to assist labor and management leaders with the development of these action plans.

A Labor/Management Foundation

T HIS FOUNDATION SERVES as the prerequisite for operating within an enlightened labor/management system. The
elements identified here are essential to the long-term growth
and success of the process.

The purpose of improving a labor/management process is
to make the fire department more effective. The focus of the
efforts is to gain the commitment of the members of the organization to the quality of services and/or products delivered internally and externally. The labor/management process assists in planning policy and developing operating procedures as well as resolving a variety of problems or issues
that arise.

▶ The fire chief and the labor leader (or union president)
must require compliance with agreements made through
the process and value participation in the process. In order to be successful, management and labor leadership

must commit to participate in planning and development processes without co-managing the day-to-day operations of the organization. In doing so, management shares authority and labor shares responsibility, or the process will simply not work.

▶ All participants have equal status in the labor/management process, but outside the process, they carry out their assigned duties in the organization. Participation in the labor/management process does not grant special privileges, nor does it relieve any participants from the basic duties of their jobs.

▶ Labor and management leaders must continually work on the issue of trust: trust in the process and trust among the individual participants.

> **Management shares authority and labor shares responsibility, or the process will simply not work.**

▶ It is okay to agree to disagree on certain issues. When this occurs, go ahead and process other areas of agreement. If labor and management disagree, yet management proceeds with a particular implementation plan, it shouldn't be represented in the organization as if it were a labor/management agreement.

▶ If labor and management make a deal, both sides must follow through. If for some reason the parties can't follow through, then they should get back together and change the deal, then proceed again.

▶ Labor and management leaders should meet and communicate regularly, deal with each other directly, and take care of problems when they are small. These leaders should talk to each other first before making a big deal out of a conflict. Always work on the labor/management relationship as well as the issues, and don't sacrifice the overall relationship for a particular outcome. The most important strength labor and management have for the future is the relationship that the leaders have with each other. It is not a secret in the fire department how the individual partici-

> The most important strength labor and management have for the future is the relationship that the leaders have with each other.

pants really feel about the labor/management process. Are they committed to the process or just going through the motions? Everyone will know and it will affect the group's ability to function together and the credibility of the entire effort.

▶ Represent the labor/management relationship for the planning and problem-solving process that it is. Leaders shouldn't take advantage of each other or abuse the process. Someone should play the role of critical evaluator to assess whether the decisions that are made within the process make sense.

▶ Guard against the need to always agree; that is not a good way to drive the decision-making process. Understand that conflict will occur. The goal is not to avoid conflict. This can lead to poor decisions and a lack of organizational

change. The goal is to provide a forum to deal with conflict through effective communications and systems.

▶ The fire chief has the final decision-making authority for
management decisions and the labor leader has the final
decision-making authority for labor decisions. This must
be understood by the participants and is a key to the effectiveness of labor/management interaction. Sometimes
a group decision is not possible or not in one (or both)
parties' best interest. In those cases, the appropriate party
should make the decision, represent it for what it is, and
go on.

If either party (labor or management) dominates the relationship, the process will deteriorate. The purpose is not to
just get along, it is to make the organization stronger by working together to accomplish common goals. It keeps the focus
of the efforts on improving the service and/or product, and
supporting the internal customers (members) who deliver or
produce it.

Defining Levels of Employee Relations and Involvement

T HERE ARE SEVERAL organizational considerations that tend to drive the degree to which relationships
between labor and management can grow and foster in the
workplace. The considerations result in positive or negative
leadership behaviors that are either complimentary or a det-
riment to moving the relationship forward. They provide a
source of guidance for establishing direction and serve as a
compass for processing conflict, which is a common element
in participation.

This book continues to dissect the root causes of confrontational and dysfunctional organizational relationships. Your
fire department's leadership might consider these behaviors
and issues within the context of your own environment and
determine the components that might be incorporated into
your specific operational model. Determining the degree to
which labor and management can find a common ground on

the following principles for involvement, participation, and problem-solving, will set the stage for a progressive, effective relationship.

Organizational principles

The following are specific organizational principals that labor and management leaders can utilize to strengthen their relationship. Although they have been mentioned previously, it is important to revisit them from a consolidated perspective.

> Quality customer service provides a joint focus for labor and management. The organizational focus must be on the internal and external customers.

▶ Quality customer service provides a joint focus for labor and management. The organizational focus must be on the internal and external customers.

▶ Traditional labor and management roles and capabilities can help achieve the goals of the organization. Each should do what they do best to improve the organization.

▶ The formal contract is very important, but it is only one component of the labor/management process. Leaders must also work on the day-to-day relationship between the two parties.

▶ Labor and management leaders must keep their word. Not doing so seriously damages what is inherently a fragile relationship. People simply distrust and lack respect for those who are not truthful with them.

▶ Joint planning and problem-solving sessions can be conducted. Smart risk-taking can be encouraged by the leadership; dumb risk-taking should be avoided to avert predictable failures.

▶ Action plans are effective in monitoring progress and keeping a work group focused and productive. Some benefits of action planning include:

- Goals and objectives are set;

- Due dates are established;

- Responsible person(s) are assigned and they report on progress achieved.

▶ Negative history must be set aside if trust is to be developed and a relationship strengthened. Dwelling on or reliving a negative past creates a substantial barrier to building strong, productive relationships for the future.

> **Action plans are effective in monitoring progress and keeping the workgroup focused and productive.**

▶ Disagreement can exist on certain issues while progress is being made on issues where there is agreement. This is sophisticated, but it is one of the key measurements of the strength and maturity of a labor/management relationship.

▶ A single issue is not worth sacrificing the long-term relationship over. The same parties will have to come together again to solve future problems. Don't solve a problem as if it's the last one you'll ever have with any participant. In a fire department or anywhere else it almost never is.

▶ Difficult times can test the relationship between labor and management leaders. Use the relationship and the process to move the organization through difficult situations.

▶ Power, control, and influence can be effectively and positively infused throughout an organization. The result can improve organizational and individual empowerment, productivity, and accountability.

▶ For participation and cooperation to be most effective, management must share its authority to make decisions with the workers, and labor must accept joint responsibility for decisions made together.

▶ The integrity and professionalism of labor and management leaders can be driven, to a large extent, by the way they represent each other inside and outside the fire department. This can define how others perceive them and impact the effectiveness of both groups in various arenas.

▶ Communications and coordination are usually enhanced when people meet to talk and listen with each other. Grievances can be rare where an active complaint and problem-solving process exists.

▶ Positive interaction between labor and management can focus the leadership on collectively solving problems and planning for the future. However, on a day to day basis, labor manages the affairs of the employee association and management manages the operation of the department within the policies and procedures that have been established. This is a critical reality within a positive fire department labor/management environment.

Committees or teams with labor and management representation are used to address issues of joint concern in many organizations. These groups can be effective if they receive appropriate guidance, support, and leadership. Their efforts should be focused on:

— Joint problem-solving

— Joint planning

— Defining the culture, and

— Developing policy and procedures

Personnel Matters
When personnel problems arise, labor and management leaders are tasked with addressing them. These leaders are human, and therefore have the capability to personalize the situation. As a result, they can become obstacles to a reasonable and appropriate solution. The following are a few principles that might serve as a guide to solutions.

▶ Managers or labor representatives who want to exercise their power rather than solve a problem become part of the problem.

▶ Punishment alone will not usually modify behavior, and tolerating unsatisfactory performance or behavior is not in the best interest of any fire department.

▶ Empathy on the part of managers and labor representatives to issues involving cultural, ethnic, or sexually sensitive complaints is critical. This is important to members and must receive the attention and support of the leadership.

▶ If possible, don't let being in a hurry allow a problem to result in a bad decision. Do what is necessary to appropriately stabilize the situation, then take whatever time is reasonable and necessary to arrive at the final course of action.

▶ We all need to improve our conflict resolution and problem-solving skills. We should seek out and attend training opportunities in these areas on a periodic basis throughout our careers.

▶ Positive, open relationships between managers and labor representatives, including early communications on issues, are very important to the process.

▶ Dealing with disciplinary matters is, in many ways, similar to any other problem-solving process or conflict resolution process. Managers and labor representatives play significant roles in both. They should follow the department's agreed upon discipline procedures when dealing with the issue of employee representation and while processing the matter to its end.

The focus of all parties involved should be on maintaining an individual's positive behavior and performance. Ensuring that *due process* and *just cause* are considered whenever a problem arises with an employee's performance or behavior is a key part of arriving at an appropriate solution. The goal of actions taken should be based on a corrective, progressive, and lawful approach to personnel actions.

The fire department should provide periodic training to supervisors covering the areas of documentation and the disciplinary process in general.

Dealing with personnel actions can be very challenging in any fire department. The primary goal whenever possible should be to return the member to a positive and productive position in the workplace. With this as a goal, labor and management leaders can focus on arriving at the appropriate outcome rather than flexing their organizational "muscles" in a way that divides all parties.

In personnel matters the stakes are high for all involved and the decisions made have a significant impact on peoples' lives and the welfare of the organization. It is important to proceed through the process with that in mind.

Relationships By Objectives

RBO: One Possible Framework

Chapter
Six

THE GOAL OF THE RBO PROCESS is to enhance the relationship between labor and management, which should be built upon trust, mutual respect, and mutual goals. Some labor/management teams began using the Relationships by Objective (RBO) process in the 1970s. Developed by the Federal Mediation and Conciliation Service, the process (see "Ten Steps" on page 40), brings labor and management together to work on mutual objectives and to discuss areas of disagreement or conflict. This relationship is used to create action plans designed to meet the needs of internal customers (employees) and external customers (those who receive the service and/or product). RBO does not take the place of the formal negotiations process (where one exists) between the employer and the labor organization.

As a component of RBO, periodic labor/management meetings or retreats are held to develop joint goals and objectives for the upcoming year. The RBO participants, a group of members from each side, document the goals and objectives in the form of action plans. Each action plan includes an achievable goal statement and objectives which can be measured and reviewed throughout the year. The action plans are assigned to one or more pre-established RBO teams to work on them.

> Each action plan includes an achievable goal statement and objectives which can be measured and reviewed throughout the year.

Follow-up labor/management meetings are held at least each quarter during the year and attended by members from each side. The purpose of the meetings is to review team progress on the action plans and to discuss current organizational issues that are of mutual interest to both labor and management.

RBO teams create a participative process within the fire department that is flexible and can respond quickly to solve organizational and operational problems. There are sometimes overlapping issues that require teams to coordinate efforts with each other.

An oversight team coordinates various team assignments and monitors achievements and progress. The oversight team is cochaired by the fire chief and the labor leader. The other teams, each representing a major area of the organization, are cochaired by a senior manager and a leader of the labor group. The cochairs of the RBO teams should make up the membership of the oversight team.

Members of the RBO teams are usually selected by the cochairs. Each team may have standing agenda items which are placed on each agenda. Teams deal with a wide variety of issues within their scope and may assign task groups to work on specific issues and report progress at meetings of the entire team. Task group membership is determined by the cochairs and usually includes members who have special knowledge or skills relating to specific issues.

Team meetings should be held at least quarterly. Each team sets its own meeting schedule and agenda to work on its assigned action plans. Teams might have other agenda items assigned to them during the year by the oversight team or they may receive suggestions from other organizational sources. Meetings and agendas are announced to the entire department in advance of the meeting and all meetings are open to any member who wishes to attend.

A labor/management operating procedure can be developed in an effort to provide more detailed guidance to the cochairs and team members regarding meetings, assignments, and the processing of issues. This helps build consistency with the operation of the various teams.

> Meetings and agendas are announced to the organization in advance of the meeting and all meetings are open to any member who wishes to attend.

Issues that are assigned to teams can enter the RBO process from either labor or management. The team analyzes each issue before they decide on a specific course of action. The team identifies the necessary level of information or training required for implementation, then reviews the results of the issue after a reasonable period of time. The review either results in revision or a decision is made by the team that no additional action needs to be taken.

The issue then becomes part of the regular routine in the department. There are times when the cochairs are not able to resolve a conflict within their team. The fire chief and the labor group leader (or union president) review the situation to determine what action is most appropriate to achieve the most desirable result. Most issues are then returned to the team to be processed.

Ten Steps for Managing the RBO Process

1. Identify the Issue

2. Assign the Issue

3. Analyze the Issue

4. Make the Decision

5. Educate as Necessary

6. Implement the Plan

7. Review for Effectiveness

8. Revise if Necessary

9. Complete the Process

10. Regroup if Necessary

1. Identify the Issue

Issues enter the process in a variety of ways. Usually, an issue comes either from labor or management, but an issue may be identified by the team, an individual member, the oversight team, management, or come from some other source.

2. Assign the Issue

The issue is assigned to a team. Assignments are received by the team cochairs. The cochairs are responsible for placing the issue on their agenda and involving the appropriate players, even if those players are not usually on the team.

3. Analyze the Issue

Issues are discussed and researched. Consideration must be given to all of the factors and resources required to achieve a positive outcome. Some of the factors include but are not limited to policy, state and federal law, city ordinances, or the formal labor contract. Research must be done on the resources required and the impact on the budget, such as personnel or staffing requirements, special equipment or supplies, or training requirements, etc.

Other considerations include the length of time it will take to complete the staff work, write specifications, develop and complete required training, or process the issue through the system. This activity requires a great deal of work and coordination between all members of the team. Alternatives are often developed and evaluated before the team makes a final decision.

4. Make the Decision

Typically the team makes the decision without going through any formal approval process. Teams work with decision-makers during the process so their decision will be acceptable to those who must manage the implementation phase.

5. Educate as Necessary

Education includes the training necessary to carry out the decision. Sometimes the team is responsible for the education phase and sometimes education becomes the responsibility of someone else. In either case, the team is responsible for making sure the education step is completed before implementation.

6. Implement the Plan

Sometimes the team will manage the implementation phase, but implementation is usually handed off to staff members. The team retains responsibility to make sure the implementation step is completed and meets the team's objectives.

7. Review for Effectiveness

After implementation, the team reviews the effectiveness of the program or project that was implemented. The team determines the length of time that should pass before it reviews the results. Their review will either indicate the need for revision or indicate that the process is complete.

8. Revise if Necessary

The team then takes the issue through the same process previously described and makes any necessary revisions based on the input they receive and any additional research.

9. Complete the Process

The process is complete when the team reviews the outcomes achieved and does not find it necessary to go through further revision. The issue becomes part of the regular routine and is managed and reviewed within the normal processes and structure of the department.

10. Regroup if Necessary

The process can break down at any point for a variety of reasons and this may require the participants to regroup. The fire chief and labor leader may decide that a specific issue needs to be reviewed by the oversight team, by the cochairs of the involved team, or through some other process. The issue is usually returned to the team. It may return in its original form with greater clarity, or may be modified so the team can effectively process it.

Summary

The RBO process works only if the leadership of labor and management want it to work. Everyone must work hard to make it successful. The most important part of the process is the relationship between labor and management leaders and the cooperation of each of the players. No single issue is worth destroying the overall relationship. Strong, effective relationships allow the RBO process to tackle and usually solve the most difficult organizational issues.

RBO requires participants to trust and respect one another, and both sides must consider each other as legitimate players. However, both sides maintain their autonomy and responsibility. They also recognize the importance of providing a process for everyone to participate at the level to which they desire. Members have their own unique point of view. The diversity of skills, talents, and viewpoints strengthens the problem-solving process and improves the quality of the service or product both inside and outside the fire department.

> Strong, effective relationships allow the RBO process to tackle and usually solve the most difficult organizational issues.

The RBO process is not designed to avoid conflict, but rather to provide a framework for processing conflict in a constructive manner. It is an excellent tool for establishing policy and procedures designed to make the organization more effective. It is not intended to interfere in any way with specific articles agreed upon in a formal labor contract or to take the place of contract negotiations.

As was previously stated, the RBO process works only when the leadership of labor and management want it to work (like so many other things in a fire department).

Evaluating the Internal Organization

THE CHARACTERISTICS DESCRIBED in this book might be much different than the organizational profile you are familiar with. Nothing in this relationship development process will replace the need for managers to possess the strong managerial skills that are required to achieve the mission, nor will it replace the need for labor leaders to be well trained and politically influential.

Taking the journey to an enlightened leadership position will not occur without significant setbacks. Some misinterpret participation for weakness; others are quick to criticize the modified and internally cooperative roles of labor and management leaders.

There are some significant components that form a basis from which to begin a general organizational evaluation. If the leadership would respond to these few basic questions, the answers might assist them in defining internal goals for an improved future.

▶ *Does your department have any descriptive literature that defines certain internal (cultural and philosophical) elements?*

▶ *Does a plan for improvement exist for the internal environment in your department?*

▶ *How does your organization's leadership act out its view of its human resources?*

▶ *Is there a big difference in the philosophy between good times (when things are going well) and bad times (when things are not going well)?*

▶ *Do you feel that the culture and values that guide your fire department are known to the membership? Are they real and alive, or simply framed and hanging on the wall?*

▶ *Has there been an attempt to provide guidance and focus to the internal and external customer service efforts of your organization? Is doing so a priority?*

▶ *Is there a process in place to enhance the quality of employee relations and involvement in your department? Are there any specific goals to do so?*

▶ *How is change managed in your organization? How are ideas managed? Can people throughout the organization input the system?*

▶ *How would you describe the level of importance placed on developing effective, lasting relationships (of all types) in your organization (by the leaders of both labor and management)?*

▶ *Are the general expectations of supervisors and other leaders defined within your department? If so, in what form? Are supervisors allowed to mistreat or be disrespectful towards employees? Are employees free to be disrespectful to supervisors, each other, or external customers?*

▶ *Is emphasis placed on individual expectations and accountability in your department? Is it understood that with empowerment must come accountability for actions and decisions?*

▶ *How would you describe the level of commitment the people in your fire department have to the department? Is emphasis placed on commending good performance or seeking out poor performers and making an example of them?*

▶ *Have you ever done a personal evaluation of yourself as a manager and leader within each of these areas? Perhaps we all should do so periodically. It is impossible to get people to practice behaviors that we as leaders are unwilling to model ourselves.*

Knowing the answers to these simple organizational inquiries can tell a great deal about the current state of employee relations in a specific fire department. As has been emphasized throughout this book, employee relations is not a stand-alone program; it is connected in one way or another to every other managerial and leadership issue in the system.

Some Final Thoughts

THIS BOOK DESCRIBES a labor/management relationship and leadership approach that is found in only a small percentage of organizations. The reason it is not more widespread is because it is very difficult and requires the setting aside of traditional roles and management techniques.

Almost everyone who teaches organizational effectiveness today stresses the importance of employee involvement, empowerment, and the forming of a partnership between management and the workers. This book outlines a road map to serve as a guide towards such an environment, but it is a very difficult and challenging journey. To take the first step, and to sustain the effort, requires the commitment of the principal leaders of both labor and management. Otherwise, it simply won't work.

Answer the many questions that are posed in this book as they relate to your current organizational environment. Consider the management and leadership concepts that are discussed as well. In developing your plan, use only the pieces of this process that make sense for your department, and don't worry about the rest for now. It is difficult to transplant this entire labor/management process into an in-place system all at once, if ever at all.

Often, too much of the collective energy expended in a fire department is directed at internal bickering, which leads to a form of infighting. This is energy that could instead be directed at improving the organizations product and/or service, and to supporting and involving the employees who make the product or deliver that service. Those who are not interested in making the organization and the people who comprise it as successful as they can possibly become should not be members of the fire department, whether they are in the labor group or in management.

It is this internal, operational partnership that forms the foundation and focus for true organizational success. How fortunate a fire department is when the leaders of labor and management see their roles in these terms and try their best to establish the relationship between the workers and management as a key organizational value. This book will help to guide you, but only the commitment and determination of the leadership will sustain the effort.

> This book will help to guide you, but only the commitment and determination of the leadership will sustain the effort.

In the competitive world we live in, if we don't travel the road together, odds are we won't get there. And if by chance we do arrive, it could be a short stay without the joint, continuous commitment of all the members of the fire department to the quality of the product, the service, and to each other. There are a few places that have figured this out, and I have been fortunate enough to work with a couple of them.

> I know the journey comes filled with doubt, so when in doubt, lead. But lead the system towards a better, more prosperous tomorrow.

This may be the most difficult organizational and leadership challenge you have ever taken on. There will be a lot of opportunities to quit and revert back to traditional, confrontational roles and actions. These will include the challenge of winning over leaders that lack the commitment and courage to change and proceed.

I know the journey comes filled with doubt, so *when in doubt, lead.* But lead the system towards a better, more prosperous tomorrow. Leave a legacy of organizational cooperation and a positive, productive, and healthy climate in which to do business. I wish you the best and hope for the sustained success for your fire department!

About the Author

DENNIS COMPTON has spent a many years designing systems and techniques to bring groups of people together in a way that fosters positive, healthy, and productive relationships and outcomes. As one colleague said, "Dennis has the unique ability to capture and simplify the keys to dealing with organizational issues, getting the most from individuals and groups, nurturing a vision, and providing a work environment conducive to individual and collective success."

Dennis has spent most of his adult life in the fire service. In a career that spans almost 30 years, he rose through the ranks to the position of assistant fire chief in the Phoenix (AZ) Fire Department and now serves as fire chief in the City of Mesa, Arizona.

Fire departments and other professional organizations have recognized Chief Compton locally and nationally for his leadership ability. Dennis has been an educator for over 20 years and has taught leadership and management at colleges, universities, private corporations, and conferences throughout the United States. He conveys a consistent message that,

> "We can study all the complex management and leadership models ever developed, but there are basic elements of organizational and individual behavior that we must address daily if these models have a chance at long term success. An organization is the people in it...it is not an abstract object. If we hire capable, committed people, support them, provide a good work foundation, apply standard management principles, communicate an enthusiastic sense of direction, and position everyone in an environment focused on the mission and on their role in meeting it, individuals and groups will behave and perform more effectively."

You'll enjoy this down-to-earth way of communicating a message that will help make you (and those around you) more effective for having learned and applied it. As a reader said, "It's a perspective and approach that's absolutely refreshing. Now let's use it to improve our workplaces, our service, and our products."

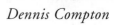

Dennis Compton

Notes

Notes

Your
Fire Service Administration
Connection

International Fire Service Training Association

We have a free catalog describing hundreds of fire and emergency service training manuals, study guides, curriculum packages, software packages, videos, NFPA standards, and informational texts for fire service administrators. Our quarterly *Speaking of Fire* magazine is also free.

Contact us by phone, fax, U.S. mail, e-mail, internet web page, or personal visit.

Phone:
1-800-654-4055

Fax:
405-744-8204

U.S. mail:
IFSTA, Fire Protection Publications
Oklahoma State University
930 North Willis
Stillwater, OK 74078

E-mail:
editors@osufpp.org

Internet:
www.ifsta.org

Personal visit:
Call if you need directions!